Dedicated to our inspiration,
Marcello.

contributions by Richard Schaedel

Jdonninibooks.com

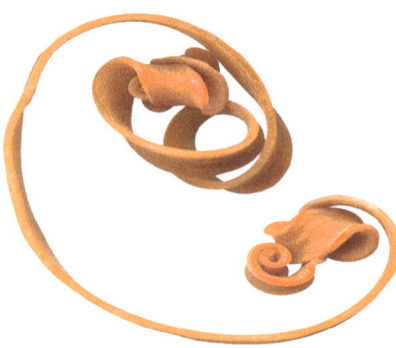

An Echo begins

in a very small Place.

But once it is born

it can reach...

Outer Space!

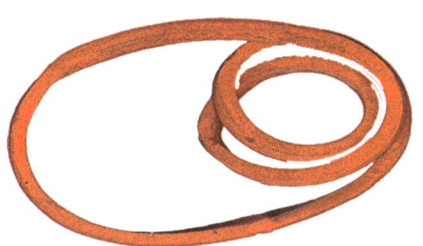

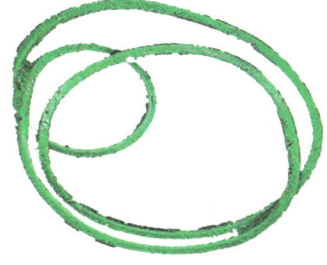

 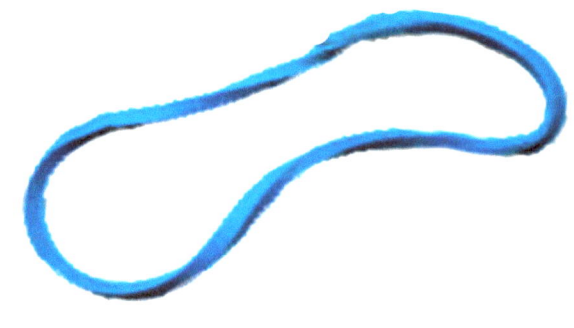

ONE becomes **TWO**

Then
THREE

Then
FOUR

BIGGER

LOUDER

until

it

reaches

a

I walk in a room.

Will anyone answer?

Hello,

are you there?

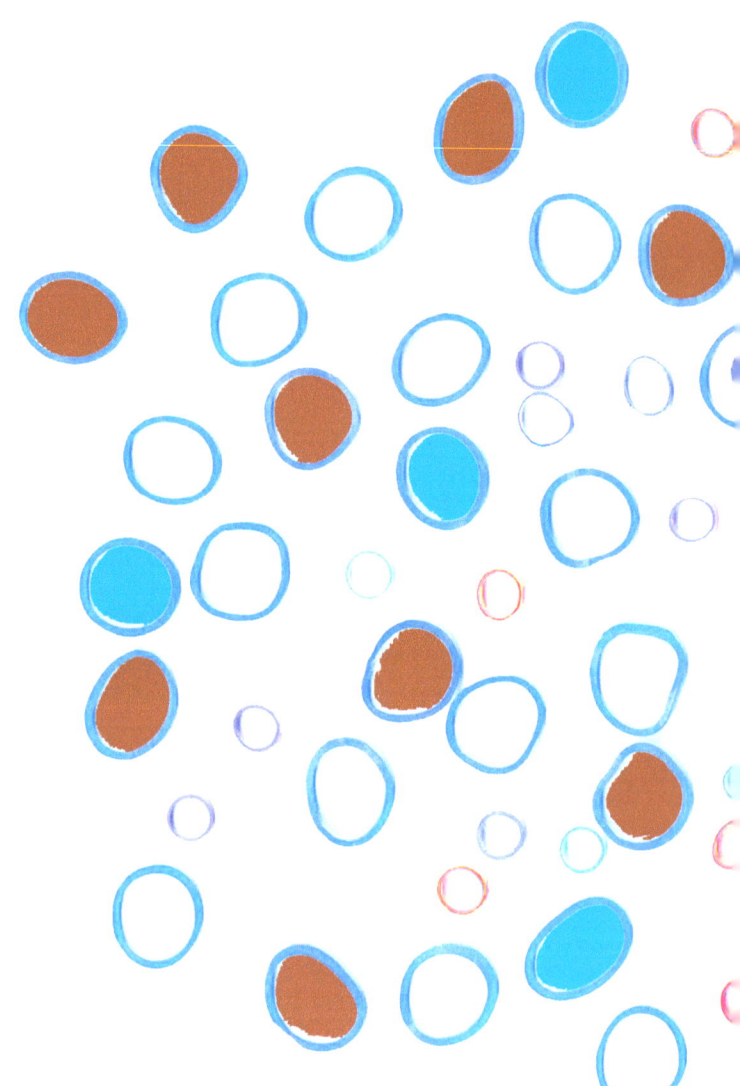

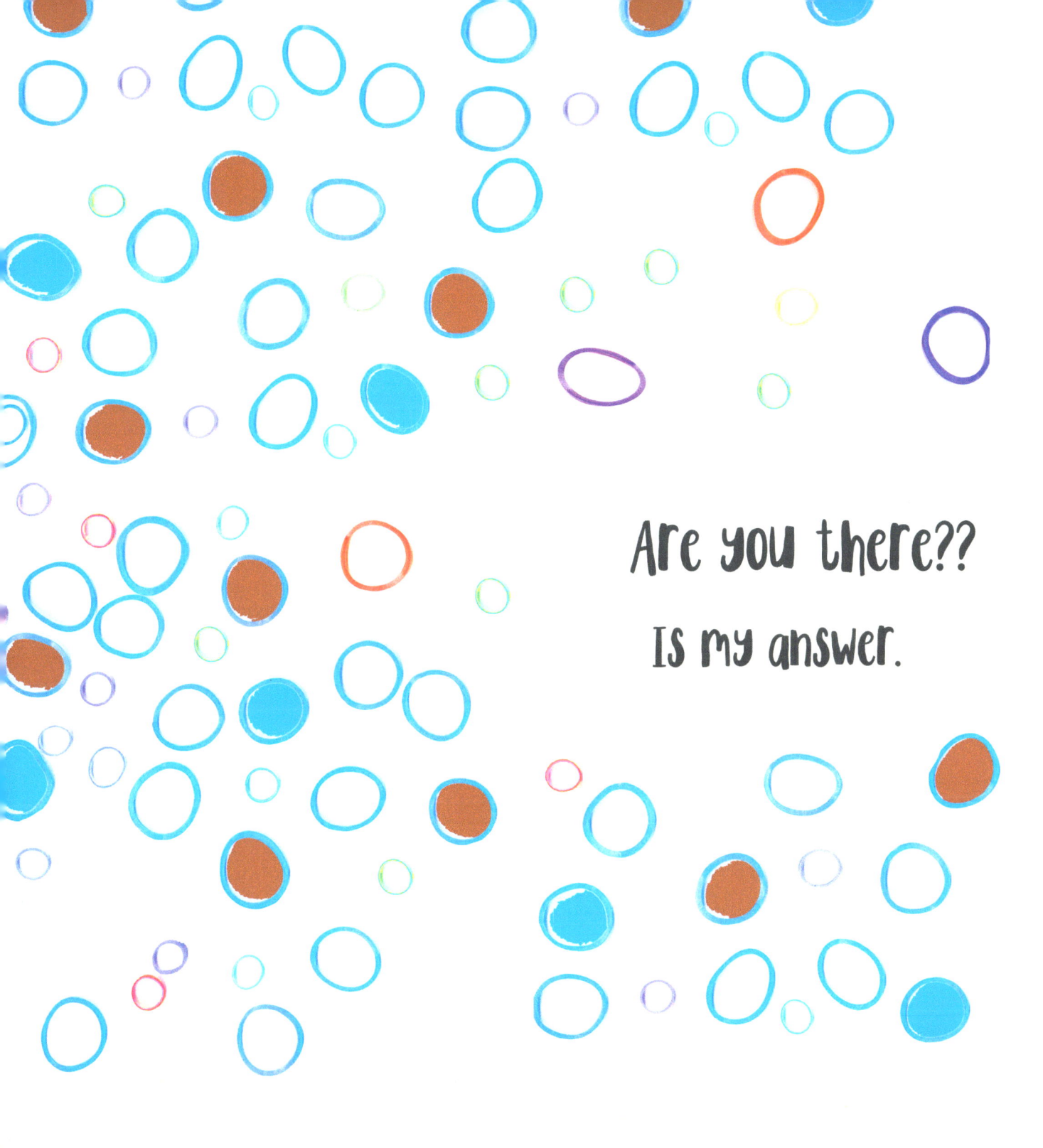

Are you there??

Is my answer.

I may be small.

But my echo is **GIANT**.
The power I have, YOU have.
So try it!

wherever you go

Test all the spaces.

Take a deep breath,

and you're off to the races!

All you need is your voice
and a curious mind
to explore this wide world,
who knows what you'll find?

So as you settle in

after a long, long day.

Can you remember

if you remembered

to Echo today?

If not....

GOOD NIGHT...

GOOD NIGHT...

GOOD NIGHT...

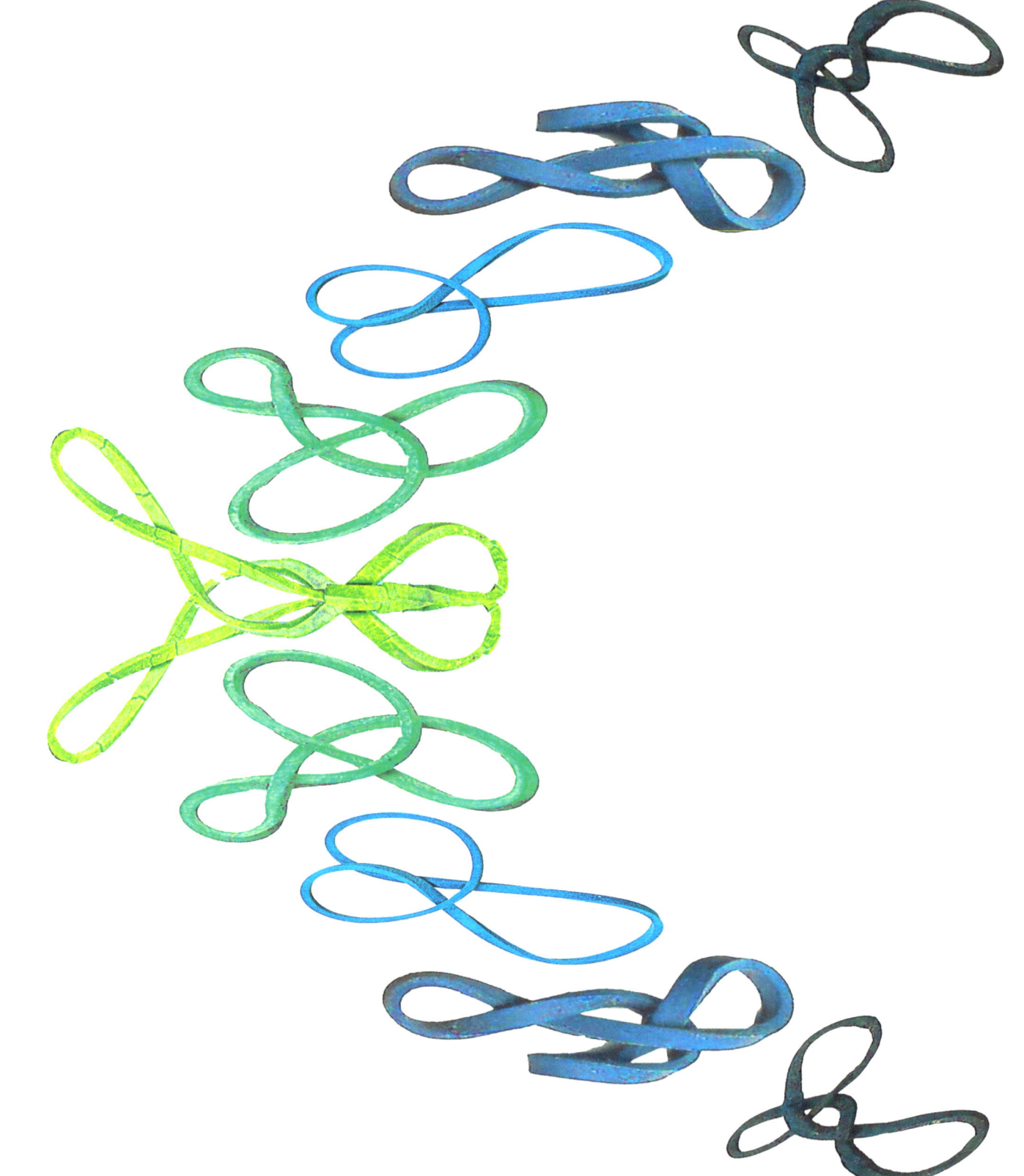

And...

SLEEP TIGHT....

SLEEP TIGHT....

SLEEP TIGHT....

What is an Echo?

When you make a sound, it travels in waves through the air, like the ripples of water in the ocean. When those sound waves reach a hard surface, they bounce back and you hear it a second time. This is an Echo.

Jdonninibooks.com

www.ingramcontent.com/pod-product-compliance
Lightning Source LLC
Chambersburg PA
CBHW041154290426
44108CB00002B/68